TED WILLIAMS

A

SPLENDID

LIFE

Contributors

Photography
AP/Wide World Photo
Allsport
Bill Nowlin

Linc Wonham ... Editor
Ray Ramos ... Designer

This book is available in quantity at special discounts for your group or organization. For further information, contact:

Triumph Books
601 South LaSalle Street
Suite 500
Chicago, Illinois 60605
(312) 939-3330
Fax (312) 663-3557

Printed in the United States of America

Contents

Introduction

I once traveled many hours into the Texas outback to visit with football Hall of Famer "Slingin'" Sammy Baugh at his ranch near Rotan, at the foot of Double Mountain. Baugh spent hours regaling me with tales about his football and baseball experiences.

One of Baugh's fascinating baseball snapshots came from a minor league game in Columbus, Ohio. "We were playing Milwaukee [then a minor league city] in Columbus, and they had a ballplayer there named Ted Williams, a young boy about 17. He played right field and he could hit the hell out of that ball. Wham!

"I will never forget, that S.O.B. would go out in right field and stick his goddamn glove in his back pocket. He'd turn his back on the pitcher on the mound getting ready to throw. Williams would be out there exercising in right field, doing goddamn jumping jacks and stuff.

"There were some old ballplayers on our team coming back down from the big league. His exercising would make these old ballplayers cuss. 'Damn,' they'd say. 'That bush leaguer. They ought to send him back down. Get him out of here!'

"They hated Ted Williams. Here was a young rookie who didn't give a damn about anything. Nothing bothered him. He'd be out there exercising, but when the pitcher would throw he'd be back around there with his glove on and be ready if he had to go get the ball.

"Then he'd come to the plate and, wham! He'd knock a goddamn board off the fence in the outfield when he hit the ball. I always wondered how that Milwaukee manager put up with that. I guess he was told to by the people above him."

Baugh recalled images of Williams once Ted had become a star with the Boston Red Sox, circling the bases during a home run, defiantly saluting the fans with the universally obscene single-digit gesture. "Williams was a screwball in a lot of ways," Baugh offered. "I thought he'd change when he got up to Boston. But I don't think he ever did."

Like Baugh, there were many in baseball who didn't understand Ted Williams' eccentricities when he broke upon the scene in the late thirties.

In that regard he heralded the age of the modern athlete—young, talented, brash, and courting conflict seemingly at every turn.

Time would reveal that the Splendid Splinter would become so much more over the course of a rich life. A marine pilot war hero. A generous spirit. A guardian of the game. A fishing Hall of Famer.

While all of these things would serve to define him, to endear him to his many fans, it was his incomparable talent, his ability to hit a baseball, that would cement all that he was. It would set him above and apart in the pantheon of baseball greats.

"There are three immediately recognizable numbers in baseball for hitters," Henry Aaron once explained. "One is Joe DiMaggio's 56-game hitting streak. One is my homer mark of 755. One is Ted's .406 batting average in 1941. When people think of streaks, they think of DiMaggio; when they think of homers, they think of me. But when they think of hitting, they think of Ted and his .406."

And they will think of Williams as long as they think of baseball. That talent, plus the brash duality of his competitive nature, strikes a chord that will ring down through ensuing generations, ensuring that Williams will be the standard by which all future hitters will be measured.

"What would he hit if he were playing today?" college basketball coaching maverick Bobby Knight, a longtime Williams friend and admirer, once wondered aloud. "Well, hell, he was 42 years old and he hit .316 with 29 homers. If Ted were playing today, the last guy to have hit .400 would not have been in 1941."

The other large part of the Williams legacy will be the enduring mystery of his personality. Perhaps no two contributors are better qualified to explore that mystery than Jim Prime and Bill Nowlin, authors of a new edition of their classic tribute *Ted Williams: The Pursuit of Perfection*, scheduled for release by Sports Publishing in July 2002. The two have spent a major portion of their professional lives studying Williams.

In addition to several other offerings about the Red Sox, Prime previously coauthored *Ted Williams' Hit List* with Williams. Nowlin is editor of publications for the Ted Williams Museum. They've researched and written countless stories about the baseball legend.

Their new edition of *Ted Williams: The Pursuit of Perfection* is a work of love, a compilation of remembrances of Ted from the famous and not so famous—everyone from Robert Redford, who contributes the Foreword, to Frank Sinatra, George H. W. Bush, and Knight, who offer their personal reflections on Williams and his milieu. Their book includes anecdotes and recollections from virtually all living members of Baseball's Hall of Fame as well as from former Red Sox teammates and opposing pitchers.

The book delves into all aspects of Williams' life: on the baseball diamond, in the skies over North Korea, and waist-deep in a salmon stream. The book also contains an audio CD featuring interviews with Williams as well as actual game calls. In conjunction with that publication, they've contributed some poignant essays on the following pages as a tribute to Williams.

In addition Nowlin has dug into his expansive collection of Williams

memorabilia to provide readers with a variety of visual images of Ted, many of them never seen before by his fans.

It all comprises a fitting tribute to a carefree young bonus baby who blossomed into a man in full, a hero for all generations, a man possessed of a talent so bountiful that he could willingly disregard it to go to war in service of his country not just once, but twice.

Perusing the following pages offers readers the opportunity to reflect on a time that has passed and a hero who will endure.

Roland Lazenby is the author of more than 45 books. His most recent is Mindgames, *a biography of one-of-a-kind coach Phil Jackson.*

Chapter

Simply Splendid

By Jim Prime

Ted Williams was a genuine American original. He possessed the fire of Ty Cobb, the charisma of Babe Ruth, the swing of Shoeless Joe Jackson, and the batter's eye of Rogers Hornsby.

But Ted was more complex than any of those men. He flew as John Glenn's wingman in Korea. He was inducted into eight Halls of Fame in various fields of endeavor. He raised millions of dollars for children's charities. He was a friend of presidents, policemen, and poets. He was America's hero and America's reflection. He was an icon and an everyman.

Williams was more than just a sports hero. Like his contemporary, Joe DiMaggio, he symbolizes an exciting but turbulent time in American life. Unlike the Yankee Clipper, though, he didn't always fit into the neat stereotypes assigned to sports heroes of his day.

Williams was a troubled hero with demons that occasionally cast a shadow over the immense talents that he brought to the game of baseball. Loud, abrasive, and brash, he was also brutally honest with the press and fans. He was driven to excel by a force so large and unrelenting that it alienated many in the very profession that should have heralded his brilliance.

They should have loved him; he was an instant cure for writer's block. But while the New York newspapers were lavishing praise on DiMaggio and deifying him in the process, segments of the Boston media chose to crucify Williams at every opportunity. The result was a love-hate relationship with the Fenway faithful.

Williams was an enigma. He lost five prime years from his career yet most experts consider him the greatest hitter who ever lived. He was accused of selfishness yet he helped countless opposing stars with their hitting and served his country with distinction in two wars. He was accustomed to the roar of 30,000 fans but preferred the solitude of fishing. He endured storms of abuse from Boston writers but probably had more beautiful words written about him than any other Boston athlete.

Simply Splendid

Gruff and often profane with adults, he doted on kids and raised millions of dollars for research into childhood cancer. He played on the last major league team to integrate and yet he was an outspoken and eloquent advocate for black players in baseball.

Wracked by injury, he batted .254 in 1959, his one mediocre year, and demanded a 30 percent pay cut from $125,000 to $90,000. He refused to tip his hat to fans during his career—even after his triumphant final at-bat—and yet fans have been tipping their collective hat to him ever since.

He was the Kid, the Splendid Splinter, the Thumper, Teddy Ballgame, and Terrible Ted. He was Ernest Hemingway, John Wayne, Paul Bunyan, Tom Sawyer, and Davy Crockett all rolled into one.

His fan base crossed the entire spectrum of American political and social influence. It included Republican presidents like Nixon and Bush, Democratic mainstays such as Kennedy and Clinton. Left-winger Robert Redford equates Williams to a Greek god and was inspired by him to wear No. 9 in the movie *The Natural*. Zen Buddhist Bill "Spaceman" Lee considers himself Williams' soul mate.

Marine Corps Lieutenant Colonel Larry Hawkins admired his sheer guts in live combat. Jack Kerouac loved his spontaneity. Frank Sinatra applauded him for doing it his way. To Nomar Garciaparra he was simply a genuine American hero, and a friend.

Williams was the American League batting champ six times, the home run champ four times, AL MVP in both 1946 and 1949 (he almost certainly deserved at least two more), and an AL All-Star 18 times. He was named Player of the Decade for the fifties by *The Sporting News*.

His lifetime batting average was .344, his slugging percentage was .634, and he hit a total of 521 home runs. His single-season .553 on-base percentage is the best ever recorded. His book, *The Science of Hitting*, is the definitive "how-to" hitting tome and has helped hundreds of young ballplayers to realize their dreams.

If any man possessed a flair for the dramatic, it was Ted Williams. In 1941 he went into the season-ending doubleheader against the Philadelphia Athletics with a batting average of .3995, which would have rounded off to .400 and made him the first player in a decade to hit that magical mark. Given the option of sitting out the final two games to preserve the average, Williams instead played both games and went 6–8, raising his average to .406.

But if hits were Ted's stock in trade, home runs were his trademark. He hit a home run in his last at-bat before going to Korea. He hit a dramatic homer in the 1941 All-Star Game to secure the American League's victory, and another off Rip Sewell's parabolic eephus pitch in the 1946 mid-season classic. And, of course, he hit a home run in his very last at-bat in the major leagues.

Home runs were Ted Williams' stage props. He employed them in the manner of a practiced magician pulling a rabbit from a top hat. They were his closing act, his exit strategy, his show-stopper, and his signature. They were his tip of the hat in lieu of the real thing.

Some homers were vaudevillian in nature. He hit one at Fenway Park that traveled 502 feet and landed on a dozing man's straw hat.

Some were melodramatic. The parting shot in his final Fenway scene in 1960 rivaled any farewell that Shakespeare could have penned. He hit homers that made fellow ballplayers stand and gape in unabashed awe. He hit line drives so sharply that first basemen feared for their well being.

Continued on page 15

Numbers Don't Lie

Ted Williams' last written words were, "I really do know how lucky I've been in my life. Get a good pitch to hit!" The words appeared in February 2002, concluding his remarks in the *Ted Williams Museum Magazine*.

The Red Sox star preached and practiced what Hall of Famer Rogers Hornsby had taught him: "Get a good pitch to hit."

Williams was sometimes criticized for taking too many walks and not swinging at pitches perhaps just outside the strike zone. But he believed if he started going for bad pitches, he'd begin swinging at ones even farther outside. It was important to maintain a disciplined approach: don't go for the ball the pitcher wants you to chase.

The primary task of a hitter is to get on base, and nobody did that better than Williams. He believed that a walk was—in many ways—as good as a hit.

In addition to putting a runner on base, he knew a walk could advance a runner and unnerve the pitcher. Williams had a career on-base percentage of .483—

in other words, he reached base 48.3 percent of the time. He walked more than 20 percent of the time—a higher percentage than any other hitter in history. He drew so many walks that his lifetime batting average of .344 (sixth best in the history of the game) became that OBP of .483, the best of any player ever.

Williams also holds the record for the best on-base percentage in a season. He had a .551 OBP in 1941, but that is about to be revised upward. Researcher Herm Krabbenhoft was preparing a paper for the Society for American Baseball Research convention in Boston the last weekend of June 2002 when he discovered two walks from late in 1941 that hadn't been included in the official record. Krabbenhoft documented his findings and Williams' corrected season mark of .553 will become the official record.

Krabbenhoft uncovered that information in the process of researching another record. He knew Yankees star Joe DiMaggio had hit safely in 56 consecutive games, failed to hit in game

number 57, and then hit in 16 more. But DiMaggio walked in game number 57, so he reached base in 73 straight games. In fact, he walked in the game before his streak started, thus compiling a streak of 74 games in which he reached base. Had anyone topped that?

After weeks of checking thousands of players' statistics, Krabbenhoft found that one hitter had topped that mark. Williams had a consecutive-games-on-base-safely (CGOBS) streak of 84 in 1949. Starting that July 1, Williams got on base in every game through September 27.

Consistency was a Williams characteristic. If games in other years in which he had only one plate appearance (as a pinch hitter) are excluded, there were only seven times he failed to get on base safely two games running. And only once did Williams fail to get on base three games in a row (May 23–25, 1939). On August 20 of that season, Williams didn't get on base in either game of a double-header. In 1940 he failed in the second game of a July 13 double-

Simply Splendid

Numbers Don't Lie

Continued from page 13

header and in the first game of the next day's doubleheader. Both days he reached base safely in the other game.

From July 14, 1940, through September 26, 1950, Williams never had back-to-back games without reaching base safely, if a couple of pinch-hit appearances in 1941 and 1948 are discounted. But on September 27, 1950, he failed to reach base in a double-header—again, his lapse confined to one day. It was nearly four years later, in September 1954, that he went two straight games without reaching base. It happened just twice more, once in 1958 and once in his final season, 1960.

There were not even many single games in which Williams failed to get on base. In 1948, excluding two pinch-hit appearances, there were only three games all season when he was kept off the bases. In 1949 it only happened five times.

Over the 292 games in which Williams appeared in those two years, there were only ten games (two as a pinch hitter) in which he didn't reach base with a hit or

walk. In 1957, soon after he turned 39, Williams reached base in 16 consecutive plate appearances:

Sept. 17 vs. KC
pinch-hit home run

Sept. 18 vs. KC
pinch-hit walk

Sept. 20 at NY
pinch-hit home run

Sept. 21 at NY
home run, three walks

Sept. 22 at NY
home run, single, two walks

Sept. 23 at NY
single, three walks, hit by pitch

SABR's Cliff Otto points out that this string includes four home runs in four consecutive official at-bats. Pretty good for an old man, who also hit .388 that year—just a handful of hits short of another .400 season. A younger, faster Williams might well have beaten out a few infield hits and made the magic mark once more.

Williams hit for power as well as average. He hit 521 home runs

despite losing nearly five prime seasons to military service. Williams was an early member of the 500 home-run club. He remains the last man in the .400 club. And he is one of the very exclusive members of the Triple Crown club, leading his league in average, runs batted in, and home runs. He earned member-ship twice, while missing by the thinnest of margins in 1949.

One would be hard pressed to find a better hitter than Williams. He achieved his child-hood dream: to have people say, "There goes the greatest hitter who ever lived."
—BN

Simply Splendid

Continued from page 12

He was the most loyal of friends and the most potent of enemies. He could disarm you with a smile or destroy you with a sneer. Somehow that fact made the smiles even more powerful.

He was a man's man but he was a woman's man too. Just ask any woman who was a teenage girl in New England during his playing career.

Was he a better hitter than Babe Ruth? Yankee owner George Steinbrenner thinks so. Was he better than Hank Aaron? Hank Aaron thinks so. Was he the best fisherman ever? Not according to former Red Sox trainer Jack Fadden, who pointed out that Jesus had produced more fish in one minute than Williams had in an entire year.

Was Ted finally humbled? Not quite. "My God," he bellowed, "You had to go back far enough to top me, didn't you?"

Usually it is the dreaded Nor'easter that hits New England head-on and catches it unawares. In 1939 a storm front in the form of Ted Williams moved in from the southwest, though it arrived more as a refreshing breeze than a hurricane.

It was only later that the skies began to darken as his lightning struck and his thunder roared. By the time Hurricane Ted was spent, he had laid waste to the record books and large segments of the Boston press.

Williams arrived in Boston from San Diego in

Williams loved to talk about hitting with teammates and opponents alike. Here he instructs another Boston player during spring training in 1958.

Simply Splendid

the spring of 1939 and within the year had captured the imagination of the entire city. His rookie campaign was an unqualified success as he batted .327 with 31 homers and a league-leading 145 RBIs, a record for freshman players.

Although the Rookie of the Year Award did not yet exist, no less an authority than Babe Ruth placed that mantel on the Kid from the Coast. In 1940 he improved his average to .344 and blasted 23 home runs out of American League ballparks.

But this was all just the color cartoon before the main feature, because in 1941 Williams set the baseball world on its ear, batting .406, hitting a league best 37 homers, and driving home 120 teammates.

With war raging in Europe, Williams played the entire 1942 season knowing that it would be his last season for a while. He signed up early in the season, did his classroom work, and still managed to win the Triple Crown. He then promptly enlisted, serving the next three years as a naval aviator and flight instructor.

When he returned in 1946, he took up right where he had left off. He led the league in RBIs for the third consecutive year and, more importantly, led the Red Sox to the AL pennant. He captured the Triple Crown again in 1947 and fell just short in 1949.

Then, just when it looked as if Ted Williams had nothing but blue skies ahead of him, he was again drafted and sent to active duty in Korea. He lost two more seasons to the military.

While in Korea, Williams' plane was hit by ground fire. He stubbornly refused to eject and successfully rode the burning craft back to base, crash landing and barely escaping in the nick of time.

When Williams returned from Korea he came back as a conquering hero and fans all across America embraced him. He got standing ovations

in all American League cities and was welcomed as a returning favorite son to Boston.

Some Williams fans argue that his greatest single year was 1957, when he turned 39 years of age. Ted batted .388 that year, winning yet another batting title.

Although unrelenting and tempestuous in his battles with the Boston writers, and occasionally with fickle fair-weather fans, Williams was always highly regarded both by teammates and opposing players. He sometimes drove Red Sox owner Tom Yawkey to distraction with the hours of free instruction he gave to opposing hitters like Mickey Mantle.

Teammate Bill Monbouquette recalls an incident in Detroit that was repeated time after time across the American League: "Al Kaline was really struggling at the plate when we came into town. Al approached Ted and asked if he could observe him in batting practice. The next thing you know, Kaline is hitting the stuffing out of the ball again—thanks to Ted. He loved hitters and hated pitchers. That's just the way Ted was. He never stopped asking questions, trying to gain any edge he could."

Even umpires looked up to Williams because they knew he was the unquestioned master of his craft. He had the eye of an eagle and he never, ever showed up an umpire by questioning calls.

Later in his life, Williams seemed to mellow—just a bit—and actually relished his role as the elder statesman of baseball, dispensing advice to rookies and veterans alike. At the 1999 All-Star Game at Fenway Park, his mere presence caused bona fide superstars to gather around him like so many wide-eyed cub scouts at the feet of Baden Powell.

But it was the real kids that the Kid loved to be around. They gravitated to him as if he were the pied piper of baseball and he never turned a child away.

Simply Splendid

Never a Doubt

It was September 28, 1941. Ted Williams was hitting .3995 going into a season-ending doubleheader against the Philadelphia Athletics. As any high school math student could tell you, that rounds off to .400 and Ted would have been the first player in a decade to achieve the mark. Little did anyone know at the time, but he would also be the last one to achieve it to date.

It had been suggested to him that he sit out the two remaining games to preserve his .400 batting average. After all, the argument went, the Red Sox were out of contention, making the games meaningless for both teams. Why risk it?

Ted was adamant. He would play. In fact, not playing was never a consideration. This was a challenge and Ted Williams lived for challenges. "I want to win it with more than just my toenails on the line," he said.

It was a cold, dreary day in Philadelphia when Williams stepped to the plate for his first at-bat of the afternoon. The Shibe Park crowd of 10,000 hearty souls had come out to see Ted Williams reach a baseball milestone. These were the true fans of baseball and they knew something special was in the air. If Ted struck out, grounded out, or hit a catchable fly ball, his average would dip below the .400 level and disaster would loom.

As Ted entered the batter's box, he received encouragement from an unlikely source. Umpire Bill McGowan, staring straight ahead as if talking to no one in particular, intoned: "In order to hit .400, a player has got to be loose."

Ted was obviously loose as he cracked a sharp single. He would get looser before the day was finished. He added two more singles and finished the first game of the twinbill with three hits in four at-bats. There was now no way he could fail to hit .400.

Surely he would sit out the second game. But Ted was just warming up. There was enthusiastic applause from the Athletics fans as Ted Williams stepped to the plate in game two. In a scene that was reenacted by Robert Redford in the movie *The Natural*, Williams hit a home run that disabled a loudspeaker in the deepest reaches of the ballpark and added a pair of other hits. He went six-for-eight for the day and ended the storybook season with a .406 batting average.

As truly significant as the feat was, the courageous way in which it was accomplished was even more significant. —JP

A Softer Side

Celebrity can be both a blessing and a burden. There are certain obvious benefits that accrue from celebrity, both to the ego and to the bank account. There are also the costs: the often oppressive expectations and demands of others, the lack of peace in public, and even the need for handlers or bodyguards.

Ted Williams suffered from celebrity to a great degree, often forced to eat in his hotel room, and often to do so alone. He enjoyed immensely being almost alone on a river or an ocean flat, with one or two friends, fishing. Yet he recognized that his celebrity could be an asset and, when the moment or the cause was a good one, he occasionally took advantage of the opportunity celebrity offered him to employ that status to benefit others in need.

Anyone who ever encountered Ted Williams knows how the phrase "larger than life" can apply to an individual. Even after Williams had been out of baseball for more than a quarter of a century, his legend seemed to keep growing.

His story was remarkable—he was perhaps the "best pure hitter" baseball has ever seen and put up some amazing totals despite five seasons lost to military service and combat duty that included many flight missions as John Glenn's wingman in Korea. Shot down once, hit by flak another time, he not only survived but came back to win a couple more batting titles and even to come within a few hits of .400 in the year he turned 39.

As a player he seemed to be embroiled in one stormy relationship after another with the press and some of the fans. With the passage of time, though, he became sort of an elder statesman of the game, more respected, his image perhaps mellowed with age.

Author's note: This article is based on research done for the book Ted and Jimmy *by Bill Nowlin. The interviews were performed by Bill Nowlin, both for* Ted and Jimmy *and the earlier book* Ted Williams: A Tribute *by Jim Prime and Bill Nowlin (Masters Press, 1997).*

A Softer Side

In part this may be credited to a better appreciation of the selfless work he did for children and other causes over the years. Though by nature media shy, Williams allowed his name and celebrity to be used to benefit New England's Jimmy Fund, raising money for children's cancer research and treatment. He devoted a lot of his own personal time as well, almost always work done out of the limelight at his own insistence.

When Williams first began supporting the work of Dr. Sidney Farber at Boston's Children's Hospital in the late forties, cancer was almost invariably fatal, particularly for children with leukemia. Diagnosis was the equivalent of a death sentence. Dr. Farber used some of the very first moneys raised to experiment with chemotherapy, more or less inventing the field at that time; he has since been regarded as the "father of chemotherapy." Today the cure rate hovers around 80 percent.

◆ ◆ ◆ ◆ ◆ ◆

"I've read about the troubled relationship that he had with the press when he was a player, and even with the fans to some extent. He's lived in his post-baseball years with such enthusiasm still for the sport of baseball, reminding people of what it was like when people worked so hard, as he did to make himself the great hitter that he was. And with loyalty to the team—all the aspects of baseball that seem missing today—it has allowed many of those minor skirmishes to be totally forgotten, and it's wonderful to just see the way he's made his way into the permanent hearts, I think, of the people in Boston, and of the media in Boston. You don't always get that in your older age."

—Doris Kearns Goodwin

Williams' biographer, Ed Linn, suggested in his book *Hitter* that much of Ted's combativeness may have been tactical. He often seemed to erupt while in a slump of one sort or another, and may well have deliberately stirred controversy as a way of getting the juices flowing. Though this may well have been true in his competitive approach to the game, there is no indication at all that his charitable works were anything other than truly heartfelt.

These days charitable activity has been institutionalized to a considerable degree in professional baseball. One of the prescribed five points that form the basis for decision in arbitration is the community work done by a player. It seems laudable that management and the player's union have agreed on this.

In Williams' day, of course, there was no union. Some teams specifically assigned charitable work to their players; others seem not to have done so. It seems clear that in the earliest years the hospital visits and fund-raising that Ted engaged in he did entirely on his own. Later the relationship between Williams' work and the team's work became so intertwined that the question of which came first made little sense.

Though Ted may have provoked confrontations with the press, and even with the fickle fans, his image in fact softened over the years; this was at least partly due to his ongoing support of the Boston-based Jimmy Fund.

Mike Andrews, former Red Sox player on the Impossible Dream team of 1967 and for many years the executive director of the Jimmy Fund, said this before Williams' death: "Ted has meant everything to the Jimmy Fund. No one is more synonymous with the Jimmy Fund than Ted Williams. The impact he has had is tremendous. He became

A Softer Side

the spokesperson, and it gave him something outside of baseball that he could attach himself to—and did he ever!

"Today he is still as interested in giving as he was as a player. In my opinion, his great accomplishment—outside of his ability to hit a baseball—is what he has meant to the Jimmy Fund. And I think he's proud of it too."

Williams said he first started raising money for the Jimmy Fund in 1947. With a span of well over 50 years, his association with the fund was the longest association of any sports figure with a given charity. It was one of the longest associations of any public figure with a charity.

Jerry Lewis has been a spokesperson for muscular dystrophy since 1952, which is a very long time. Only Bob Hope, in his relationship with the USO, seems to have a longer span. Hope did his first USO tour in 1942.

In recent times, we have seen Elizabeth Taylor as a spokesperson for AIDS research, and a few other figures in the entertainment world who have lent their names and time over a period of years to specific causes. That Williams devoted himself so fully to the Jimmy Fund for over half a century, however, has to be one of the greatest legacies of a storied life.

The Jimmy Fund effort began in earnest with a fund-raising appeal that grew out of a national radio broadcast of Ralph Edwards' *Truth or Consequences* on May 22, 1948. The broadcast featured a phone link from Hollywood direct to the hospital bed of "Jimmy"—a youngster ill with cancer at Children's Hospital in Boston. The audience was told, without Jimmy listening, that he was very ill but wanted a TV set so he could follow his favorite team, the Braves. As Edwards chatted with Jimmy, various

members of the Braves team came one by one into Jimmy's hospital room and presented him with gifts—balls, bats, even a uniform. It was a dramatic and touching story and, within hours, people were driving to the hospital in person with cash gifts. Mail contributions flowed in and $250,000 was quickly raised, providing an excellent start for Dr. Farber's fund-raising efforts.

Jimmy was always kept anonymous, and everyone (including Jimmy Fund staff) assumed he had died some time later. Much to everyone's surprise, the original Jimmy, one Carl Einar Gustafson, reappeared on the eve of the 50th anniversary of the broadcast in time to join in all the celebrations of what had been accomplished over the decades. Gustafson is a healthy father and grandfather today and now makes appearances for the Jimmy Fund, when not busy with his profession as a long-distance trucker.

The original broadcast, along with a number of local New England events it directly inspired, raised nearly a quarter of a million dollars for Dr. Farber's work on cancer in children.

The Boston Braves were the first team sponsor, but when the Braves left town for Milwaukee in early 1953, the Red Sox took over, and it was Williams more than anyone else who picked up the ball, launching a major effort when he returned to Boston and to baseball following two years with the marines in the Korean War. Boston's Variety Club, a group of theater owners, has been active since the very beginning, and they were able to bring in many Hollywood stars to help them with the film trailers, but clearly it was Williams who was the most consistent draw.

Bing Crosby, John Wayne, and a host of other Hollywood celebrities cut film trailers for the Jimmy

A Softer Side

Fund. Ronald Reagan and others have come to Boston to help raise money as well. When you hear the remarks they have made, it becomes clear that they themselves may only have become interested because this was Williams' charity. It is impossible to calculate the sum total of all of Williams' efforts.

Williams' support was not just the mere lending of his name, though he gave the Jimmy Fund carte blanche to use his name in any way they deemed helpful. Ted personally served in many capacities over the years, making countless appearances at restaurant banquets and drive-in theaters, posing for check presentations at Fenway Park, traveling all over New England for the Jimmy Fund, and offering as an additional incentive to donors his signature as the endorsement on checks made out to the Jimmy Fund.

Clearly Williams took the Jimmy Fund a quantum leap forward when he began in earnest in 1953, knowing that the Braves had left town and being willing to take it all on his own shoulders. With the support of the Yawkey family, owners of the Red Sox, Williams gave the fund the momentum it needed to carry it into and well through the sixties.

Carl Yastrzemski was one player who carried the banner forward in Boston after Ted had moved away. When the Red Sox won the pennant in 1967, Yaz successfully urged his teammates to vote the Jimmy Fund a full equal share of the proceeds from the extra income.

In more recent years, Red Sox players such as John Valentin and Mo Vaughn have become closely identified with the Jimmy Fund. Throughout, though, Williams kept coming back to Boston and continued to grant the Jimmy Fund that carte blanche privilege.

When Williams was inducted into the National Baseball Hall of Fame in 1966, the Jimmy Fund was pleased to be able to announce that some 120 persons had contributed $250,000 to it in his honor, and that a special plaque would be displayed at Cooperstown.

"Throughout his playing career, even while he was being lambasted by sportswriters as a mean SOB, lousy father and husband, and selfish showboat, Williams plugged away at the Jimmy Fund, and those of us who loved him as a player could take comfort in knowing that this was the real Ted, the great-hearted Ted."

—John Updike

Ted always took a particular interest in kids. Ed Linn writes, "Most of his high school teammates have a story about some handicapped kid whom Ted befriended. The kid with the harelip, the kid with the bad leg, the kid who stuttered. One of the things George Myatt had found most attractive about the wisecracking 17-year-old just out of high school was his unfailing instinct for the underdog. 'Even then, he was doing things for old people and kids.'"

During his minor league year in Minneapolis in 1938, the first year he spent away from home, Ted visited kids in local hospitals on several occasions, as newspaper clippings from the day attest. This was the sort of thing certain ballplayers did back then. Babe Ruth was known for visiting kids who were sick, and Williams may have picked up on that, but it was almost certainly deeply ingrained in him through the daily example of his mother's devotion to the unfortunates of Tijuana and San Diego.

In June 1939, shortly after Williams had first arrived in Boston as a 20-year-old rookie, he again responded to the particular call of a child in the

A Softer Side

hospital. Williams received a letter from a West Roxbury, Massachusetts, carpenter named George Nicoll, who at the time was employed as a cafeteria cashier. Nicoll asked if Ted could visit his son Donald, 11 years of age and dying of peritonitis. The boy was at Faulkner Hospital in Jamaica Plain.

Ted wrote back and agreed to visit. "The first kid I visited in Boston, a boy named Donald Nicoll, was dying of a stomach disease," Ted wrote in *My Turn at Bat*. "I got a nice letter from his dad, saying they were fans of mine, asking me to visit the boy. I still see the family. The boy made a great recovery. . . . An awfully nice boy."

Donald Nicoll's appendix had burst, and the doctors believed there was no hope he would survive. Nicoll's father, a real sports fan, was excited that Williams was going to visit. "Who's he?" Donald recalled responding.

The boy recovered and today lives in Portland, Maine, where he is retired but still keeps active as

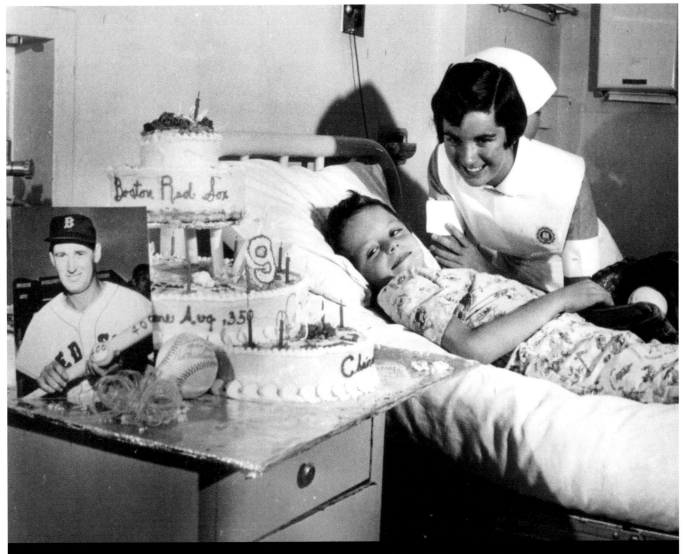

Williams devoted much of his life to bringing happiness to sick children and their families.

A Softer Side

a consultant to nonprofit organizations. "[Williams] came to visit me once or twice subsequently at the hospital, and then came to our house [over] the next couple of years," Nicoll remembers.

Clearly, it can be terribly depressing to visit so many fatally ill or seriously injured children over the years, but Williams persisted as though it were a calling. Perhaps in part influenced by his mother's devotion to social service, perhaps just enjoying the kids and knowing that a simple visit could bring some joy into their lives and those of their troubled families, Williams soldiered on.

"Certainly I have seen some pathetic cases," he once recalled, "some pitiful, sorrowful things." He mentioned visiting several children who had lost limbs to train accidents, electric shock, and fire. Then there were the Jimmy Fund kids, wasting away from childhood cancer.

Williams devoted himself to Dr. Farber and the Jimmy Fund from the late forties right into the new millennium. If he had wanted to do charitable work simply to look good, for the benefits of public acclaim, he could have picked a less wrenching cause. There are plenty of good causes for which one could make perfunctory appearances. There would have been no need to immerse himself with suffering and dying children and their families. Given both his reluctance to have his private visits publicized and the nature of the cause he selected for his primary involvement, it seems indisputable that his was a sincere calling.

Williams characteristically shifted the focus from himself to those who worked for the children. "I know I am just one of a multitude of athletes who have gone to see kids in hospitals, to see sick kids," he wrote. This kind of contribution, he continued, "is so overrated compared to what the people *in* these hospitals are doing. I have always felt that it was just a twist of fate anyway that I was allowed to be on the outside, strong and healthy, instead of in there with them, maybe in a wheelchair."

Williams had everything needed to make a great athlete, and the will and perseverance to put it all together. Stephen Koster, son of the Jimmy Fund's first executive director said to a *Boston Globe* reporter before a Jimmy Fund tribute to Williams in 1988 that Ted "is a huge man with terrific athletic abilities, and then there's a little kid lying in a hospital bed unable to do the hundreds of thousands of things Ted could do. It touched him deeply. He wanted to do something to help those kids, and he found the Jimmy Fund."

Al Cassidy, a businessman who ran the Ted Williams Baseball Camp for kids in Lakeville, Massachusetts, and was always zealously protective of Williams' privacy and confidences, reflected for a moment: "If you like Ted Williams, and you want to be his friend, you grant him refuge. The Jimmy Fund gave him that much. He has allowed that his name be used in any fund-raising capacity, and he has made speeches and appearances, but he did not want credit for visiting a kid in the hospital. It was like heaven when he came walking into a house. Not only for the kid he was visiting, but for the whole family. It was a tremendous burden on the family. These kids would usually be terminal. They wouldn't have too much time left. He walks into a house of average means and, gosh, that kid would just, you know—he couldn't believe it. All the kid could do was lie in bed and listen to the radio, and here comes Ted Williams into his room to see him.

A Softer Side

"I'll be damned if one of the guys once called the *Boston Globe* about his visit," Cassidy recalled. He told the *Globe's* Ian Thomsen, "Your paper was going to be there with a photographer and everything. [Ted] heard that and he said, 'No, we're not going to do it,' and that was that. After the event passed he said, 'Come on, let's go,' and then he went to the hospital.

"[When he visited the child in privacy] he'd set up the camera and sit with the kid and say, 'Let's take a second one in case the first one doesn't turn out.' That was the real Ted Williams."

Nowhere in the files of the Jimmy Fund is there a photograph of Ted Williams visiting one of these children in his or her room. Keeping his visits private suited Ted's personality. He was if anything embarrassed by all the attention he received.

Brian Interland, a record promotion man and former partner in Grand Slam Marketing and the Ted Williams Card Company, says, "Ted gave more of himself than anybody that I've ever seen in my life. He always did. You know about the children in the hospital with leukemia. He did a lot of things that nobody ever knew about, because he cared. He never lost that little kid in him. That's one of the great things about Ted. People might find fault in it but it's amazing that with that little kid in him, he related to young kids and has a feeling for young kids that very few people [can truly capture].

"Babe Ruth might have had that same thing. Somehow Ted relates better to them. It's that little kid in him. Maybe it was when he was a kid, being he didn't have the home life, there might be something. . . . Still, to this day, he just seems to light up, melts, when he sees a kid."

"I was eight years old when Ted Williams played his last game in the major leagues, but I have been fortunate enough to become acquainted with Ted over the last decade. Ted's nearly lifelong involvement with the Jimmy Fund is as much a part of his legacy as .406, and yet another reason to admire and respect him."

—Bob Costas

Mort Lederman has been at The Jimmy Fund for 45 years, currently serving as manager of general services and the director of security. "It was a summer job that's lasted for 45 years," he says. Lederman first met Williams in conjunction with the Jimmy Fund during the late forties.

"There are a lot of celebrities that I'm not crazy about. When you work here all your life . . . I met everybody—Muhammad Ali, President Reagan, Prince Charles. Ted, though, was somebody that impressed me like crazy," recalls Lederman. "He impressed me because he was a very sincere . . . no bull----, sincere guy.

"A lot of these baseball players come over, 'Well I gotta do it, in and out . . .' He was a really sincere person; he was really dedicated. Ted was a very, very bright gentleman. Very articulate. He didn't thrive on publicity; it didn't mean anything to him, to look around to see who's watching. He was as private as could be."

"Unlike most celebrities," Lederman told Linn, "Williams never had a demand. . . . He was a backdoor guy, and I admired him for that."

When the occasion called for him to meet with dignitaries, though, Williams excelled. "He was very handsome when he was young. He had this

A Softer Side

charisma. When he'd walk in the room you knew Ted Williams was there. He was loud and big; you knew he was there."

Asked if he recalled the time when John Wayne and Ted visited the Jimmy Fund together, Lederman did: "I'm 6'2", and Ted Williams is 6'3". When I got on the elevator with John Wayne, because my job is to meet these people, he looked like a big, big, big, towering ghost. I thought I was a big man. He was the biggest man I've ever seen. I was the only one there to see John Wayne come

Williams, who did his best to keep his good works out of the public eye, was on hand for the 1988 unveiling of Ted Williams Highway outside of Boston.

up to Ted Williams, when Ted put out his hand and said, 'I'm Ted Williams.' And John Wayne said, 'Heard about you, boy.' "

Linn, in his biography of Williams, writes, "What Williams took on himself was the agonizing task of trying to bring some cheer into the lives of dying children and, perhaps more difficult, comforting their parents. Over the years he permitted himself to become attached to thousands of these kids, knowing full well that he was going to lose them one by one. He became so attached to some of them that he chartered special planes to fly to their deathbeds. Obviously these were not token visits. He knew most of the patients' birthdays and as much about their backgrounds as possible. When he was about to meet a new patient, he would rummage through the child's mail while the child was in the examining room in order to find some personal way of reaching out to him.

"The most difficult thing in the world, as any adult knows, is to communicate with children at their own level without being patronizing, Ted had no trouble at all. He would come into a ward like a warm, friendly puppy and remain exactly that way until he left, a big child among little children.

"Ted worked so hard for the fund, getting out of a sickbed on occasion to make a scheduled appearance, that it is obvious he must have been getting something very fundamental in return. When the question was put to him directly, however, Ted, who was normally loud and articulate, became vague and uncomfortable. 'Look,' he said, 'it embarrasses me to be praised for something like this.

" 'The embarrassing thing is that I don't feel I've done anything compared to the people at the hospital who are doing the really important work.

A Softer Side

It makes me happy to think that I've done a little good. I suppose that's what I get out of it. Anyway, it's only a freak of fate, isn't it, that one of those kids isn't going to grow up to be an athlete and I wasn't the one who had the cancer?'"

With all of the ways in which Ted Williams contributed, it is quite possible that he even made an impact on national policy at the highest levels of government. Sidney Farber spent 20 years lobbying Congress for his plan to "construct a network of regional treatment and research hospitals throughout the country, and it was this plan that became the model for President Richard M. Nixon's War on Cancer.

Dr. Farber lived just long enough to see his dream become a reality. As he said: "Don't overlook the possibility that Ted might have played a role in it. Ted and Nixon were great friends. When Nixon was vice president, he would come to the Statler almost every time the Sox were in town and have lunch with Ted in one of the hotel's private dining rooms."

Said Williams himself: "Next thing I know I'm in Washington, and the next year he's president of the United States. He was a pretty good baseball fan. He was only five minutes from the ballpark, and he'd come down for the last five or six innings with Julie and David Eisenhower, then come to the clubhouse to see me after the game."

Did Ted lobby for his dying friend, Dr. Farber? "I can't recollect, to be honest, that I sat down and talked to Nixon that way, but certainly it was always brought up somewhere around my conversation. Every place I went in those years I talked about it. You'd work all year, and you might raise a million and a half bucks, and you'd need three or four million. It was very, very important that we get those donations in New England because the federal government was giving us matching funds.'"

Williams is a baseball legend and a military hero. He's been described as the man John Wayne tried to portray on the screen, the "real John Wayne."

He was a major national figure in his day, on the cover of dozens of magazines. He is still front-page copy in New England, and has had a few highways and now a tunnel in Boston named after him. He's been inducted into a few sports Halls of Fame, both as a baseball player and a fisherman, and was the first living athlete to have a museum created in his honor.

He did a number of endorsements, most notably Sears after his retirement and, ironically (both given his work for the Jimmy Fund and the fact that he himself never smoked), even for a couple of cigarette companies in the late forties.

He could have exploited his celebrity for personal aggrandizement. Instead of hitting the lecture and banquet circuit for himself, though, he chose to do it for others. There are many stories about things Ted did, financially or otherwise, personally or anonymously, on a one-on-one basis for people who needed assistance, friends and strangers. The Jimmy Fund was not the only cause he helped, though it was the greatest recipient of his energies.

The research pioneered by Dr. Farber at Children's Hospital in the treatment of cancer was the first real breakthrough and those accomplishments continue right through to the present time.

Ted Williams was one of the greatest hitters, if not the greatest, in the history of baseball. He also pitched, extensively and consistently, for the Jimmy Fund in the long effort to strike out cancer in children.

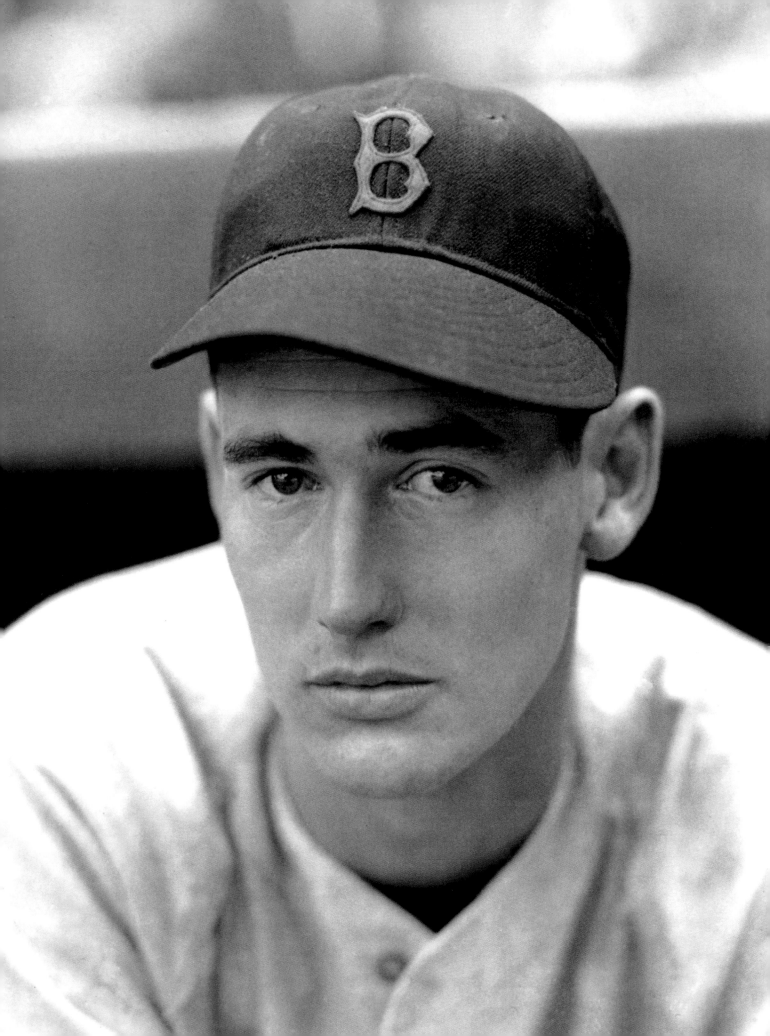

Proud Heritage

By Bill Nowlin

Pedro Martinez? Nomar Garciaparra? Luis Tiant? If the question is: "Can you name the preeminent Hispanic player in Red Sox history?" there can only be one answer.

Ted Williams.

In February 2001 in San Francisco, Williams became the first inductee into the new Hispanic Heritage Baseball Museum Hall of Fame. Williams' Latino pedigree surprises many, but the Splendid Splinter was always private about family.

In his 1969 autobiography *My Turn At Bat*, Williams acknowledged his heritage as "part Mexican" and recognized the difficulties that might have been his lot. He wrote, "If I had had my mother's name, there is no doubt I would have run into problems in those days, [considering] the prejudices people had in southern California."

I grew up in Boston and Ted was my hero. A seven-time batting champion, he is considered by many to be the greatest hitter ever to play baseball.

After I married into a Mexican-American family, I became intrigued that the hero of my youth had Mexican ancestors. Many questions begged for answers: Was he shaped by Latino culture in any way? Did he share special friendships with other Latino players? Why does it seem that his Mexican background was virtually a secret?

My Turn at Bat gives Williams' mother's name as May Venzer, but when I began investigating in 1999, I couldn't find any Venzers in the phone listings for California, where Williams grew up. However, a photocopy of Ted's birth certificate showed her name as Venzor. It was misspelled in his book!

Here was a thread to follow, though the real breakthrough came in an e-mail from one of Williams' cousins, Manuel Herrera, who had read a book on Williams that I had coauthored.

Herrera explained in a later telephone interview that the Venzor family, especially Ted's uncles in Santa Barbara, had a significant but unpublicized influence on his life. Ted's maternal grandparents were Natalia Hernandez and Pablo Venzor. The family was Basque in origin and had settled

Proud Heritage

around Hidalgo del Parral and Valle de Allende in the state of Chihuahua, Mexico.

Natalia and Pablo were married in 1888. As political troubles began to brew in Mexico, they joined the exodus north to Texas. Ted Williams' mother, May, was born in El Paso in 1893, one of nine children. The family later migrated west to Santa Barbara.

May married Samuel Williams around 1915, shortly after the groom was mustered out of the military, and the couple moved to San Diego, where Ted grew up bearing his father's Anglo surname.

In a 1999 telephone interview, May's younger sister Sarah Diaz told of frequent family visits back and forth between Santa Barbara and San Diego, where she often looked after her young nephew. Were it not for Diaz, Ted would often have been home alone as a boy. In his autobiography, Williams wrote that his mother was "gone all the day and half the night, working the streets for the Salvation Army. I didn't see much of my dad."

Still, May Williams managed to take her son to visit family in Santa Barbara, 200 miles away. Diaz told me, "Ted loved to hunt. He loved to fish. My

Left to right: Pete Venzor, Saul Venzor, Natalia Venzor, and Paul Venzor

father was a good fisherman, and all my brothers used to go out here on the wharf in Santa Barbara and fish."

But the first sport of the Venzor family was handball, a sport rooted in Basque tradition. And Ted's uncle Ernesto Ponce—one of the last family members born in Mexico, in 1913—was a great handball player. For many years he was the tristate handball champion of Texas, Arizona, and New Mexico.

Ponce lives in El Paso now, and when I visited him in 2000, he said, "I played baseball, just as a kid. I never played on a school team or anything, though. I was a pitcher, because my expertise was handball. Several of my mother's brothers played handball, *pelota*. When he was a young kid, Ted liked me. He'd always look at my hands and say, 'I want to be just like you.' These were the hands of a handball player. Big. Rough. We never talked baseball back then."

"I loved handball," Williams told me when I visited him at his Florida home in 2000. "I wasn't the best I've ever seen, but I was pretty good." And besides Ponce, he went on to mention two of his

Continued on page 32

Proud Heritage

Leading by Example

Ted Williams surprised many people when he took the occasion of his induction into the National Baseball Hall of Fame to call for the recognition and inclusion of Negro League players. To those assembled to honor him, Williams declared, "I hope some day Satchel Paige and Josh Gibson will be voted into the Hall of Fame as symbols of the great Negro players who are not here only because they weren't given the chance."

To those who knew him, the only surprise may have been that he made such a public pronouncement of what had been his practice throughout his life. Williams was never a crusader, but he lived his life as a believer in merit, regardless of race or background. He also always had sensitivity to the difficulties facing other men.

In accepting a Brotherhood Award at Howard University in 1971, Williams said, "As I look back on my career, I'm thankful that I was given the chance to play baseball; it's about the only thing I could do—and I've thought many a time about what would have happened to me if I hadn't had a chance. A chill goes up my back when I think I might have been denied this if I had been black."

Larry Doby was the first African-American ballplayer in the American League, entering baseball just 11 weeks after Jackie Robinson broke the color barrier in the National League. Williams didn't make a big show of it, but he gave encouragement to Doby, a dozen years before the Civil Rights Movement.

Doby remembers, "When I first got in the League in '47, he was one of the few people who said 'hello' and 'good luck.' The thing that impressed me about Ted is that . . . with some people you can feel sincerity. With other people, you can feel it was politics or something. He was just a quiet kind of person, going about his business. Didn't have to make any big deal out of it. That's why I feel it was from the heart. He wasn't grandstanding, but just making a fellow player feel welcome on the field."

Williams apparently also had taken the time to send a personal letter to Jackie Robinson shortly after he crossed the color barrier in 1947. Rachel Robinson, Jackie's widow, said, "Jack was very impressed that someone of that stature took the time to do that. That was the kind of person Ted Williams was."

Ironically, the Red Sox were the last major league team to integrate, at long last bringing Elijah "Pumpsie" Green up to the big league club in 1959. Williams never made a speech about it; again, he led by example. Howard Bryant, in his book *Shut Out*, explains. "If Pumpsie Green was unsure of what to expect from his teammates, Ted Williams provided the answer," Bryant writes. "The great, aging star chose Green to warm up with him before every game. It was the symbolic gesture of a true leader, for even if anyone did harbor a problem with Green's arrival, no one would cross the mighty Williams."

Bryant later caught up with Green in California and asked him what he thought when he heard Williams' Cooperstown speech. "He remembers smiling to himself. He remembers Ted as one of the few players that first year that made him feel like both a ballplayer and a man."   —BN

Proud Heritage

Continued from page 30

mother's brothers: "Pedro, he was a damn good handball player. And his brother Saul was a damn good athlete."

In fact, it would be Ted's uncle Saul Venzor and the sport of baseball that would make the strongest impressions on young Teddy Williams. One reason the homegrown summer game appealed to him was the proximity of San Diego's North Park playground to the Williams home on Utah Street. The other was the skill displayed by the first baseball players in the Venzor family, who mastered the game and played it with fiery determination.

Much credit has been given to North Park playground director Rod Luscomb and others who worked with Teddy as he drove himself relentlessly to become a better baseball player. But some of his earliest instruction, and his single-minded determination to excel, came from his own family, his uncle Saul, who played semipro ball and managed one of the local semipro teams, the Santa Barbara Merchants.

Sarah Diaz recalled Ted's visits to Santa Barbara in the early thirties, when he was a teenager: "Ted played with my brother Saul. We had a big garden, and they'd get out there and throw the ball to each other. Ted learned a lot. When Ted would come, the first thing they would do is get out there in that field and pitch to each other and bat. My mother was left-handed and, boy, she didn't miss when she threw rocks at us to get our attention."

Ted, his mother May, and younger brother Danny

Saul Venzor was stubborn and aggressive. He was tough on Ted. Manuel Herrera said of Williams' uncle: "He really had the tools, and Teddy would literally beg Saul to teach him how to pitch a baseball. No one could beat the guy and he hated to lose. Saul gave Ted more than just pitching lessons. He used a 'no-lose' attitude to build Ted's confidence and [taught him] how to think and win. Not just get the ball over the plate, but to think with your head and always be aggressive."

Recently, Santa Barbara baseball organizer Tim Badillo, 91, called Saul Venzor one of the best pitchers around during that time. "He was a great prospect when he was a young man," said Badillo. "He could throw a ball through a wall! He played semipro for quite a while, and he played with one of the leading Mexican teams [Union Protectora Mexicana] in Southern California."

Proud Heritage

Herrera recalled, "Ted would plead: 'Uncle Saul, can I pitch now?' Saul said, 'Aw, you're not ready, kid. Maybe you're not hungry enough.' 'Oh, please, uncle Saul!' He'd tell Ted, 'Oh, maybe another day. Not today.' 'Oh, come on, uncle Saul! Please!' He'd beg him all day. Ted would throw his glove down and walk out of the room."

In the eighties, when Williams was visiting Saul Venzor's widow, Henrietta (Venzor died in 1963 at the age of 60), she recounted this very story. Williams listened with a big grin on his face. The young Ted's determination to prove himself as a ballplayer to his uncle Saul helped form the resolute drive that later made him such an outstanding ballplayer.

Another cousin, Frank Venzor, confirms Saul's role in molding the youthful Williams: "Saul was the one who started this baseball stuff, who got Ted into baseball. The slanted driveway on Chino Street looked like a pitcher's mound. Saul and his brothers used to put Ted up at bat. 'Get up there. See if you can hit this,' they would yell at him.

"They were not nice to him. Ever. They used to tease him. He'd be out there bawling and crying. They'd get him out there on the driveway and he'd be crying. 'Get closer! Get up there! See if you can hit this!' My uncle could throw. He could throw 19 different pitches. This is where Ted began to recognize them. My aunt used to stick her head out the window and say, 'Saul! Leave the kid alone!'"

Williams' mother moved fluidly between Anglo and Mexican communities in her work. Her Santa Barbara clan fit into the local Anglo community, although family members still enjoyed their traditional *carne asadas*, or backyard barbecues.

The oldest generations—Williams' great-grandmother Catarina Hernandez and grandmother Natalia Venzor—spoke only Spanish, but Williams spoke only English.

Joe Villarino, who knew Williams since grade school and often played baseball with him in those days, describes himself as Mexican. He was born in the same neighborhood as Williams, and his family, like Williams', was eager to assimilate. Consequently, Joe also never spoke Spanish growing up, despite having a Mexican father and a mother from Spain.

Joe understood that his friend Ted never identified as Mexican. "He never did. Not that he didn't want to be known as a Mexican, but it just wasn't part of his life."

Although he did not turn his back on his Basque-Mexican heritage, Williams, a very private man, was uninterested in—or uncomfortable with—talking about either side of the family. Williams was brought up Anglo, with an Anglo surname; he entered a world of baseball where he may have hit against a Camilo Pascual and a Pedro Ramos, but they were just pitchers, and he was just a hitter.

Did Williams ever develop special friendships with Latino players? It doesn't appear so, but in recent years Nomar Garciaparra became one of Williams' favorite players. In February 2001, a couple of weeks before the Hispanic Heritage Baseball Museum induction, I asked Garciaparra if their mutual heritage had ever come up in conversations with Williams.

Nomar laughed, and said, "Yes. He said to me, 'You know, I'm Mexican as well. My mother was Mexican.' I said, 'God, Ted, I knew I liked you!' We just joked around about it."

—*Bill Nowlin*

An American Hero

By Bill Nowlin

When John Glenn boarded Discovery to return to space late in 1998, Ted Williams boarded a helicopter to travel to the Kennedy Space Center at Cape Canaveral to witness the historic launch. Two of the true heroes of our time were both former marine pilots and they enjoyed a friendship going back nearly 50 years.

They first got to know each other during a frigid winter at the desolate air base at Pohang during the Korean War. Both aviators flew combat missions, sometimes together, and both narrowly escaped death. Ted's plane was hit by ground fire on two occasions and Glenn's was hit a full dozen times.

The experience they shared created a bond that lasted over the years, despite one being a Democrat and one a Republican. Williams, despite giving three years to military service in World War II, was called back to active duty at the age of 34 (and consequently had another two years taken from his playing career with the Red Sox). Although not pleased about having been reactivated, Williams complied and then gave it his best.

In the Second World War, Williams had flown and—being exceptionally good at both flight and gunnery—been assigned to train other pilots. However, he never saw combat. Korea gave Williams the chance to fly jets for the first time. This offered the chance to master a new craft, a thrill in itself. It also gave him true combat experience, which added to his legend as an American hero, not just a baseball star.

Marine Captain Theodore S. Williams completed training and landed in Korea on February 4, 1952. He was one of 32 marine pilots in squadron VMF-311. When he first entered the squad room, one of the very first people he met was a pilot from Ohio named Glenn.

"When I first got there, I didn't know anybody so I went to the pilots' room just to get acquainted. I looked over to the other end of the room and I saw two marine majors there. I didn't know who they were, but they looked good to me. One was John Glenn."

An American Hero

Williams had arrived one day after Glenn. "I think I first met him at Cherry Point going through jet refresher," recalled Glenn. "I didn't know him well there. When we got to Korea, though, I was assigned as operations officer of the squadron out there, VMF-311. Ted was assigned as my wingman and flew with me. That didn't mean that every single mission you went out on you flew with exactly the same person, but it meant that if you're both on the schedule going to go up a certain day, those two people would go up together. I guess probably half the missions that Ted flew in Korea he flew as my wingman. You get to know that guy pretty well."

Williams flew 39 missions in Korea, and Glenn flew 63. It was a fighter-bomber squadron and both flew F9F Pantherjets. The F9F carried 1000- and 2000-pound bombs, 50-mm machine guns, and 20-mm cannons. "Those were missions involving bombing, strafing, rocket firing, and napalm drops on enemy targets," explained Glenn.

"You fly as a two-person element. We call it a section. That means two planes, and then your next flight formation is four planes. You put those two sections into a division as it's called, and then build on up to a squadron from there. Your two people stick together and if you're going into combat, they fly together and if there's air-to-air combat, then you watch out for each other and you fly back and forth together.

"We were doing a lot of close air-support work and things like that, with napalm and bombs on the ground and rockets and so on. And if somebody

Williams and future astronaut Glenn (opposite page) flew dozens of missions together in Korea.

An American Hero

got hit then you stuck with him, you stuck with that guy, and you made every effort to get him back. It was that type of situation. We were under intense antiaircraft fire on almost every mission. By the time we got out there, which was in late '52 and then into '53, it was a rare mission you went on when you didn't see antiaircraft fire."

These were true combat missions. Glenn talks about one such mission with Williams: "On one mission we were assigned an area where we thought they had ammunition stored. Well, one of the best things that ever happened on a mission like that was if you got a good hit and got right into the bunkers, their ammunition would start going off. That's what you call a secondary explosion. The

first explosion was from the bomb. The secondary explosion was when all their stuff on the ground started going off.

"I went in on this run and got a good hit and it was blowing up on the ground. Ted was coming right in behind me and he pulled out of his run right behind me and he yelled on the radio he'd been hit, he'd been hit.

"Under the right wing tip was a good-sized hole. He still had the airplane under control and there wasn't any problem so we flew on back and landed. What had happened was he'd had a rock blown up from the ground on a secondary and hit him in the tip tank. We always kidded him about the Williams antiaircraft fire.

Williams signed himself back into service as an active reserve in May 1952.

An American Hero

"We did a lot of flying. On some of the more memorable missions, we were doing road reconnaissance. You'd take off real early in the morning, before dawn, before there was any first light even, and you flew up at altitude. You'd be way up north, oh, maybe 150 miles or so up behind enemy lines, and then you'd let down, just at first light when you could see enough that you could come down and skip along on the roads flying at real low level. One plane would fly down there and the other plane would fly along about 1,000 feet along behind and direct the first plane on the ground to make a right over the next ridge or so on to keep him on the road and you'd shoot up any trucks and things like that.

"I remember some of those, a couple of those flights with Ted in which he and I flew together. I'd fly down low for 10 minutes or so and hit whatever targets I could and then we'd switch off and he'd fly low, and you'd switch off back and forth and work your way back down to the front and come on home."

Williams almost had his career cut short after 10 seasons in the majors. He still would have been the last man to hit .400. He still would have had his two Triple Crowns, a feat only Rogers Hornsby has ever matched. Williams only barely missed having three.

He still would have had an exceptional career, but he would have wound up with just 324 home runs had he been killed in Korea. On one bombing mission early in his combat duty, Williams' plane was hit badly and he was forced to land at another base, crash-landing his jet and escaping from the smoking F9F just as it burst into flames.

Williams had, during training at Willow Grove, Pennsylvania, witnessed an F-9 that had crashed by the base and burned. He watched as they pulled body parts out of the wreck.

On one of his earliest missions in Korea, while dropping antipersonnel bombs on enemy troops, his plane was hit by small arms ground fire. "When I pulled up out of my run, all the red lights were on in the plane and the damn thing started to shake . . . I was in serious trouble."

His radio conked out. Williams was sure he was going to have to bail out, and worried because with his tall frame, that would be an almost certain (and very serious) knee injury—not to mention landing in ice-cold waters or in enemy territory. He'd said, "It was the only real fear I had flying a plane, that if I had to bail out, I wouldn't make it. I thought I'd surely leave my kneecaps in there."

Another pilot, Larry Hawkins, flying behind Ted, found him going off course and caught up to him. Hawkins steered him back in, giving hand signals to the radioless Williams. Hawkins had no idea it was Ted; to him it was a marine aviator in deep trouble.

Hawkins, who retired a lieutenant colonel, recalls the story: "The day Ted crash-landed his jet, he was well ahead of me, probably about a mile and a half. As I was coming up off the target after dropping my bombs, I was pulling up and heading west, toward the Yellow Sea. That's when I spotted this aircraft going toward the north/northwest and I said to myself, 'That guy's going in the wrong direction.' Then I spotted the puffs of smoke coming out. I flew up alongside and looked over at him, and he looked over at me, but I didn't know who it was.

"I saw this puff of smoke, this puff, puff, puff, these gentle puffs of smoke coming out of the tail section. Well, I soon found out, it wasn't hydraulic fluid. As we went along, it continued to stream and that's when it dawned on me it was fuel. I thought, 'We've got a problem.' He must have been hit either in the main fuel cell or somewhere in one of the fuel lines.

An American Hero

"He had no radio. So it was just hand signals. I just patted my head and I said, 'I'll take the lead,' and so he followed me. I went out to the Yellow Sea and then I turned him south/southeast, following the coastline. I set him up over the airfield—King-13—just south of Seoul. Suwon was the name of the air force base. So we circled around and I set him up at 7,500 feet, and I pointed down to the airfield. He looked and I'm sure he caught the picture because 7,500 feet at a certain spot in the air was part of the flameout pattern. Had he flamed out—you know by this time, I figured if he's lost all that fuel—he'd have to deadstick it or eject, one of the two.

"I gave him the 'wheels down' signal, which was a standard signal for that particular pattern. There's a standard pattern for a flameout pattern. He put the wheels down and, as soon as he dropped the gear, the damn wheel well doors blew open. And of course by this time we were slowing down where we'd be under 200. We were down somewhere between 150 and 170 knots. And he broke on fire.

"So I hollered over the air, forgetting that he had no radio. I said, 'Eject! Eject!' Well, he didn't hear me, but he got the picture that something had gone wrong. So he slapped the gear handle back up. By this time he was burning slightly. As the gear came back up, the fire just kept smoking, there wasn't that much fire coming out of him. We turned back to the field at about 180. He was about 3,500 feet, something around there. They cleared the runway and then he came screaming across the end of the runway, doing about 200. I was, oh, about 150 feet in the air. He hit down, and by the time he slid 5,000 feet, 5,500 feet or so, I saw the canopy go off, and I looked over my shoulder and there I saw this big tall figure scrambling out of

that cockpit and running to the side of the runway. I never saw a guy move that fast in all my life."

Williams said he was coming in quick for a landing when there was a big explosion in his plane and "one of the wheel doors had blown off. Now there was smoke and fire underneath the plane. Why a wing didn't go was just an act of God. . . . With 30 feet of fire streaming from the plane, the villagers were running to beat hell. . . . For more than a mile I skidded, ripping and tearing up the runway, sparks flying. . . . The canopy wouldn't open at first, then I hit the emergency ejector, and the fire was all around me, everything on fire except the cockpit. Boy, I just dove out, and kind of somersaulted, and I took my helmet and slammed it on the ground, I was so mad. There were two marines right there to grab me. I came back and looked at the plane later, and it was burned to a crisp."

John Glenn wraps it up, the way he heard it: "Ted got hit and was coming back and there was smoke coming back and all this business and I don't think he . . . as I recall, he couldn't hear the radio transmissions, that was out.

"He knew he was on fire and didn't want to get out, and he was just lucky. He brought the thing around and couldn't get the gear down and bellied it in and it slid up the runway and he jumped out of the cockpit and ran off and stood there and watched it melt down. He was just lucky the thing didn't blow."

Williams guessed that when he landed he had only 20 or 30 seconds worth of fuel left. It was probably this very lack of fuel that saved him from having his entire Pantherjet engulfed in a fireball.

Jerry Coleman of the Yankees had also been called up and sent to Korea. "We were on that mission, the whole marine air was up in North Korea

An American Hero

that day. We were listening to this as it developed. We had no idea what happened in the end. We had no idea at all it was Williams until a day or two later."

Had Ted Williams been killed, we would have lost one of our greatest ballplayers midway through a stellar career. The Jimmy Fund would have lost the man who, immediately upon his return from Korea, became its biggest fundraiser. Baseball would have lost the advocate who converted the occasion of his own induction into the Hall of Fame into a plea for recognition of the black ballplayers who had not had the same opportunities as he had. America would have lost a towering personality who went on to touch and inspire countless thousands (fans and others) with his words, deeds, and example.

Williams was back up and flying the very next day. That's the way it was done. Williams looked for no special treatment in Korea. He slept in a hut with the other men, on "a bed one of the guys had made—a major who was going home. It was two two-by-sixes, three feet apart, and the springs on it were the rubber inner tubing off a jet's tires. It was all bent up, curved on either side from being squeezed together so long."

Glenn, once more, asked to evaluate Williams overall, concluded, "He did a great job and he was a good pilot. He wasn't out there moaning all the time or trying to duck flights, or anything like that. He was out there to do the job and he did it. He did a helluva good job."

The Ultimate All-Star

By Bill Nowlin

Even "The Greatest Hitter Who Ever Lived" made outs most of the time. Still, as a veteran of 18 All-Star games, Ted Williams compiled an enviable record in the midsummer classic.

He had two spectacular games that provided two of his proudest moments in baseball history. Playing all out, he seriously hurt himself in a third game. He played injured in a couple of others, taking unnecessary chances with his career.

In some respects, All-Star Games aren't meaningful games. They're an honor for the players—and these days a number of players have incentive clauses that pay them a bonus for making the squad—but the results mean nothing in the pennant race.

Consequently, some devoted baseball fans regard the All-Star Game with a bit of a ho-hum attitude. Many of the players take the All-Star Game seriously, though, particularly in decades past when players stuck with a team and were typically an American Leaguer or a National for their entire playing career.

"I always enjoyed the All-Star Games," Williams wrote in his autobiography. "[I liked] getting a chance to see the other league's great pitchers, seeing a Koufax or a Drysdale or a Robin Roberts, finding out what I could do against them."

There's no doubt that Williams was excited about his first All-Star Game. Coming off a spectacular rookie year in which he knocked in a record 145 RBIs, he was a natural for the team. The manager was teammate Joe Cronin, and other Sox players Jimmie Foxx, Doc Cramer, and Lou Finney all traveled to St. Louis with Williams.

But it wasn't a memorable game for Ted. He walked in the first, grounded out twice, and was replaced by Hank Greenberg late in the game. The whole AL team only mustered three hits against a dominant National League pitching staff.

The 1941 game in Detroit, midyear in Williams' .406 season, was the game that Ted always said provided the biggest thrill of his long career. Williams walked in the second, then doubled in a run in the fourth. He flied out his next time up, in

The Ultimate All-Star

the sixth. The Cubs' Claude Passeau struck him out in the eighth on a called strike, one that Ted thought was a bit low.

Jimmie Foxx reported that for a couple of weeks Williams had been saying that he wanted to hit one out, but it wasn't looking like a truly special game for the young star. The AL was behind 5–3 in the bottom of the ninth, and the bases were loaded. Joe DiMaggio grounded a ball for a fielder's choice and knocked in one run.

Williams was up for the fifth time in the game now, with runners on first and third and two outs. Passeau was on the mound, hoping to strike Ted out once again. Not too many pitchers struck Williams out twice in a row, though.

The first pitch was a ball. Williams fouled the next one down the first-base line. Then came ball two. There was a pretty strong wind blowing across the field, but Williams hit Passeau's next pitch off the front of the press box built on top of the third deck, nearly out of Briggs Stadium, for an ending Hollywood couldn't have topped—coming from behind, with two outs in the ninth, to win the game 7–5.

We've all seen the film of Williams galloping around the bases, clapping his hands as he ran, laughing and smiling. The *Boston Globe* reported that "hardened veterans like Joe DiMaggio, Bob Feller [already changed into street clothes but

out on the field to greet him], Joe Cronin, and Jimmie Foxx were suddenly transformed into boyish hero worshippers."

Williams never stopped running until he reached the dugout, an act perhaps of self-preservation as he was mobbed both by his fellow teammates and spectators who ran onto the field. "I just shut my eyes and swung," he said. "I had a feeling that if I got up there in the ninth, I'd go for the Downs. Boy, I feel good. There ain't nothin' like hittin' a home run. . . . Do you know the biggest kick I got out of the whole thing? I'm tickled for my mom's sake because she was listening."

This was a side of Williams not that much appreciated in later years, as he fought to keep his personal life private. That evening after his triumphant home run Ted chatted with a reporter who'd stopped by his hotel room. He went into the closet and brought out the letter he'd received from his mother the day before. Williams read parts of her letter out loud in which she wrote about how proud she was that he'd made the team.

He continued talking, not about his game-winning homer but about a great throw he'd made (a "tremendous heave," according to news reports) that had prevented a run from scoring earlier in the game.

The Ultimate All-Star

The next year, in 1942, Ted faced Passeau yet again. The only Red Sox player on the team this time, Williams was so anxious to repeat the feat from the year before that he uncharacteristically swung on a 3–0 pitch and flied out. He went one for four with a single and three fly-outs. The "stormy string-bean slugger" was a mere mortal once again—though by the time the year was out Ted Williams had won the Triple Crown.

Off for three years in military service, the only All-Star action he saw was a 1945 "All-Star Baseball Series" at Furlong Field in Pearl Harbor, where a team of American Leaguers (including Johnny Pesky, Bob Lemon, Fred Hutchinson, and Bob Kennedy) faced a National League team that fielded Stan Musial, Cookie Lavagetto, and others.

The Red Sox won the AL pennant in 1946, and were such a dominant team that one third of the All-Star squad was from Boston that year—for the first All-Star Game ever played at Fenway Park. Dom DiMaggio, Bobby Doerr, Rudy York, Hal Wagner, Pesky, Williams, and pitchers Mickey Harris and Dave Ferriss were all selected. The Sox could have fielded every starting position except third base.

Passeau—still a great pitcher—was the NL starter. He worked very carefully on Williams and finally walked him on a 3–2 pitch. One could argue that it was the only damage Williams didn't do all day—but a walk's as good as a hit and Ted was on base for Charlie Keller's home run.

The AL began building what became a 12–0 shellacking of the National Leaguers. Williams hit a solo homer his next time up, singled in the fifth to knock in another run, singled again in the seventh, and then homered for three more RBIs in the eighth.

That final home run was the first anyone had ever hit off of Rip Sewell's famous "eephus pitch"— a pitch thrown with a roughly 20-foot-high trajectory that came down over the plate. The Pirates' Sewell saw Williams as a challenge, saying of the Splendid Splinter, "He just loves to bat. He doesn't walk up to the plate. He runs up to it."

The first pitch Sewell threw was an eephus, which Williams fouled to third. "That was my fist look at the eephus or the oophus or whatever you call it," Williams said. "I stepped back and tried to push [it] to left."

A fastball followed: strike two. The third pitch was another eephus, way outside. Williams correctly anticipated the next pitch. "I stepped into it and gave that last one all I had." He strode forward, coming out of the batter's box in his eagerness.

"The ball took about five minutes getting up there, and he had plenty of time to think it over," remarked Tex Hughson. Williams hit it into the bullpen in right, where pitcher Mickey Harris caught it.

Williams went four for four with a walk, two singles, and two home runs for 10 total bases. The rest of the team together accounted for just 14 more. It was one of the greatest displays of hitting in All-Star history, and in front of the home crowd to boot.

Joe Gordon borrowed one of Williams' bats in the seventh. "See, I'm goin' to use Williams' bat," he announced. "I'll show it to the pitcher first, label up, so that he can read the name and he'll be scared to death right away." Gordon hit a double high off the wall in left-center, barely missing a homer himself.

Bill Dickey grabbed a Williams-model bat too, but took a called third strike. "Even the wood in a Williams bat is no good," he allowed, "when the stick is on your shoulder."

The Red Sox won the pennant that year, but lost the Series in seven games. Williams suffered an injury shortly beforehand but gamely played

The Ultimate All-Star

throughout the Series; his performance suffered. One Cardinal pitcher, Harry the "Cat" Brecheen, held Williams to just one hit in nine at bats.

Williams got a bit of revenge against Brecheen in the 1947 All-Star Game, going two for two with a single and a double. He was two for four in the game. One of the outs was a called third strike, and the following year umpire Jocko Conlan apologized to Williams for missing the right call.

Williams was unable to start the 1948 game due to rib cartilage that had torn loose in a game in Philadelphia. He did pinch-hit in the sixth and drew a walk.

The 1949 game was unremarkable, with Williams coincidentally suffering from a cracked rib. He was hitless in two at-bats but got himself on base twice, drawing another couple of walks. Ted also made a great over-the-shoulder catch that "helped save the game," according to Lou Boudreau.

The 1950 game came close to ending Williams' career, and cut short what could have been a tremendous season. Ted was off to his best start ever, with 25 home runs and 83 RBIs before the All-Star break.

Williams made a great catch in left off Ralph Kiner in the first, snagging the ball over his shoulder and then crashing hard into the unpadded wall at Comiskey Park. The first edition of the *Boston Globe*, composed while the game was still in progress, had a full-page headline: Williams' Spectacular Catch Robs Kiner.

Williams made another difficult catch off of Kiner a couple of innings later. At the plate he grounded out, flied out, singled to drive in a run in the fifth to put the AL team in the lead, and struck out looking in the seventh.

Williams played the whole game until he was taken out, now in considerable pain, in the ninth. He'd actually broken the radius, near his elbow, but gritted it out and acquitted himself well. It was two months before he could come back after the operation back in Boston.

In 1951 he went one for three with a triple and a walk. Called to military service once more, Williams did not play in either the 1952 or 1953 games. Just home from Korea, though, Marine Captain Williams attended in uniform to throw out the first pitch in the 1953 contest.

The 1954 game saw Williams strike out twice, a rare phenomenon for any game. He also drew a walk. Williams was one for three in the 1955 All-Star Game, with another walk. Willie Mays ran down and snared a long ball that would have gone out.

Williams played in seven more All-Star Games (two were held each year in 1959 and 1960), but, with the exception of a home run off Warren Spahn in the 1956 game, he did nothing particularly special. In 16 plate appearances those last seven games, he got the one homer and singled once, walking just twice.

The single, slashed hard to right field, was a pinch-hit in his final All-Star appearance, in 1960. Before that final game, at Yankee Stadium, Williams was given a great cheer that the *Boston Globe* described as "reminiscent of the famous farewell salute Boston fans gave Yankee Joe DiMaggio several years ago in Fenway Park."

All told, Ted Williams batted .304 in All-Star competition (excellent, but not compared to his lifetime .344 total) with four home runs and 12 RBIs. Disciplined at the plate as always, he drew 11 walks and so increased his on-base percentage to an impressive figure of .431.

CHAPTER FIVE

The Ultimate All-Star

The Ones That Got Away

On more than one occasion, Ted Williams paid the price for his prickly relations with the press. How can a ballplayer win the Triple Crown (leading the entire league in average, home runs, and RBIs) and not be named Most Valuable Player? Someone else was more valuable?

What if that happened not just once, but twice? What if the ballplayer led the league in home runs, slugging, on-base percentage, runs, walks, and hit .406, while the actual MVP winner lacked in every category and was a full 49 points lower in batting average, at .357?

Williams may have played in 18 All-Star Games, but think of how many league MVP awards he could have snared. By almost any objective standard he was deprived of the award four times he should have won it. The reason: the sportswriters he so disdained applied subjective standards and ranked Williams lower—in one case not even including Williams in the top 10 players in the league.

In 1941 the Kid hit .406 and he also led the league in home runs (37 to Joe DiMaggio's fourth-place 30, slugging (.735 to DiMaggio's second-place .643), on-base percentage (.551 to DiMaggio's third-place .440), runs (135 to DiMaggio's second-place 122), and walks (145—almost double DiMaggio's meager 76.)

New York's DiMaggio led the league in RBIs (125 to Williams' 120) and had his famous 56-game hitting streak. His average was .357 and Williams' was .406. But DiMaggio was from New York, and the Yankees won the pennant handily that year—and he didn't yet attract the negative press that Williams did.

Then came 1942. With war under way and controversy swirling around him, Williams embarked on a season of base-ball during the day and four hours of military classroom work in the evenings. He won the Triple Crown but Joe Gordon—also of the New York Yankees—walked off with the Most Valuable Player Award.

Williams didn't just lead the American League in all three categories, he led both leagues. That had only been done three times before—by Ty Cobb in 1909, Rogers Hornsby in 1925, and Lou Gehrig in 1934. Gehrig led both leagues in 1934, though by just one percentage point in average.

And Williams didn't just lead in those three categories, but in several others as well. He led by such margins that he left the competition in the dust. In all, consider this chart:

Statistic	Williams	AL runner-up	NL leader
AVG	.356	.331 (Pesky)	.330 (Lombardi)
HR	36	27 (Laabs)	30 (Ott)
RBI	137	114 (DiMaggio)	110 (Mize)
OBP	.499	.417 (Keller)	.417 (Fletcher)
SLUGGING	.648	.513 (Keller)	.521 (Mize)
TOTAL BASES	338	304 (DiMaggio)	292 (Slaughter)
RUNS	141	123 (DiMaggio)	118 (Ott)
WALKS	145	114 (Keller)	109 (Ott)

How did Williams stack up against Joe Gordon?

Statistic	Williams	Gordon
AVG	.356	.322
HR	36	18
RBI	137	103
OBP	.499	.409
SLUGGING	.648	.491
TOTAL BASES	338	315
RUNS	141	88
WALKS	145	79

Williams led the league in average, home runs (twice as many as Gordon), runs batted in, runs scored (by a huge margin over Gordon), bases on balls (almost double Gordon's total), on-base

The Ultimate All-Star

percentage, slugging percentage, and in a number of more newly formulated statistical measures not cited here.

Williams' figures, except for batting average and home runs, were distinct improvements over his 1941 figures, and he was only down by one homer. Gordon, on the other hand, "led the league in nothing but errors and strikeouts," as one observer once remarked.

Actually Gordon's 26 errors only placed him seventh worst in the league—though he did lead all second basemen in errors. Gordon's fielding percentage of .966 was not nearly as good as Williams' .991. Gordon did lead the league in strikeouts by a healthy margin, whiffing 95 times. He also led the league in grounding into double plays, with 22.

In 1946, the year the Red Sox coasted to the AL pennant, a deserving Williams won the MVP. The team that wins the pennant does seem to have an edge in MVP voting.

In 1947 Williams won the Triple Crown again, but once again lost out to Joltin' Joe DiMaggio, who in King Kaufman's words, "wasn't even as close to him as he had been in '41, which wasn't very close." DiMaggio led the league in nothing but fielding average that year.

Statistic	Williams	DiMaggio
AVG	.343	.315
HR	32	20
RBI	114	97
OBP	.499	.391
SLUGGING	.634	.522
TOTAL BASES	335	279
RUNS	125	97
WALKS	162	62

Did the baseball writers vote objectively or subjectively? Williams won the MVP again in 1949. Perhaps the writers suffered a bit of guilt after 1947 and decided to give him another shot. He deserved it—he came within a fraction of a

percentage point of winning a Triple Crown a third time. If he'd had one more hit, or George Kell had one less, Williams would have three-peated as a Triple Crown winner.

Lou Boudreau had won the year before, but Williams stacked up well. In fact, Ted led Boudreau in runs, homers, total bases, RBIs, walks, average, on-base percentage, and slugging. Boudreau didn't lead the league in anything, except fielding percentage. But his team did win the pennant (in a one-game playoff against the Red Sox, Boudreau himself practically single-handedly making the difference) and Boudreau was Cleveland's key player. At least here, one can't argue that Williams was robbed.

Williams had another strong year in 1951, but the Yankees' Yogi Berra won the MVP. Williams led the league in many categories while Berra didn't lead in any. New York took the flag and another New York Yankee won the MVP.

Ted went to war for a couple of years, then had a few solid years that were years when other players truly were better. In 1957, though, the year Ted turned 39 years old, he had a tremendous season—and Mickey Mantle won the MVP award. The Yankees' Mantle led the league in runs (123 to Ted's 96) and walks (146 to Ted's 119), but Ted topped The Mick in average (.388 to .365), in OBP (.528 to .515), homers (38 to 34), and SLG (.731 to .665).

If Ted was just a bit faster, he might have beat out five or six more hits and batted .400 once again. He was that close. But the MVP award, once more, went to the best player on the team that won the pennant.

Even in 1958, at age 40, Williams won the batting championship, his six and last. There were several legitimate MVP candidates that year: Mantle, Colavito, and the actual winner, Jackie Jensen. Williams could equally well have deserved the award.

The years 1941, 1942, 1947, and 1957, though, seem to be ones in which Ted truly did post better numbers than the man awarded the MVP.   —BN